The soul should always stand ajar
ready to welcome
the ecstatic experience.

Emily Dickinson

OTHER BOOKS BY CELESTE SNOWBER

In the Womb of God: Creative Nurturing for the Soul
Liguori, 1995

Embodied Prayer: Towards Wholeness of Body, Mind, Soul,
Wood Lake/Northstone, 2004

Landscapes of Aesthetic Education co authored with S. Richmond,
Cambridge Scholars Publishing, 2009/2011

Wild Tourist

Instructions To a Wild Tourist from the divine feminine

Celeste Snowber

**Silver Bow Publishing
Box 5 – 720 – 6th Street,
New Westminster, BC
V3C 3C5   CANADA**

Copyright © 2016 Silver Bow Publishing
Cover Painting: "JUMP UP" Dobee Snowber
Layout/Design: Candice James

All rights reserved including the right to reproduce or translate this book or any portions thereof, in any form

Library and Archives Canada Cataloguing in Publication

Snowber, Celeste, 1956-, author
    Wild tourist : Instructions to a wild tourist from the divine feminine / Celeste Snowber.

Includes index.
Poems.
ISBN 978-1-927616-19-2 (paperback)

    I. Title.

PS8637.N713W54 2016   C811'.6   C2016-900101-6

    Email: info@silverbowpublishing.com

    Website: www.silverbowpublishing.com
    Website: http://www.alibris.com/stores/silverbow

preface

This is not a book I was planning to write. Wild tourist took a hold of me and wrote itself out of the depths. Its conception was on the Big Island of Hawaii in Kapa'au on the Kohala Coast. I was awoken in the middle of the night as I had a habit of doing; and had very interesting conversations with Pele, who is the Hawaiian volcano goddess. Yes, it sounds a bit wild, but then this is nothing new for me. I am a wild woman who loves to knit. I have lived in my own contradictions of wildness and domestication for many years. I was on an artist holiday/retreat, and yet there was nothing about sedate which I experienced. I was being enlivened once again from the inside out, and this book came. I listened, and I wrote; and I kept listening and wrote more.

I offer it to you as a vehicle to re-awaken the creative one within you; the glorious one who sings in the night, dances in the day, and drinks from the unpredictability of what resides within. The mystery of the feminine divine, found in Pele alerts us to the place of wide-awakeness. One can call being wide-awake many things, but the essence is the same. I invite you on a journey to uncover the interior, wild heart through a releasing to all of the senses. May you pick this up and put it down, and let it accompany you through the seasons of your life. See it as a loving friend who speaks to you when you are out of rhythm, and calls you home. Home to the exquisite place of you; the only you there is. And here is raw joy, and the raw material for living your delicious life from the inside out.

Table of Contents

you are the earth	9
wildness	11
plans	12
maps	13
signs	14
living exotically	15
the terrain of your own flesh	16
a tourist in your own life	17
a bagless life	18
raw joy	20
where is she	22
the body sings	23
what about	24
one orange	25
wired from the inside out	26
I am enough	27
inner mardi gras	30
hair or no hair – let it down	31
live out loud from a deep place of silence	33
ripe tomato	34
limits & liminality	35
fertility	37
dreams & dreaming	38
dark chocolate	39
tears	40

living into the not yet	41
rehearkening	42
riot of color	43
in-between of travelling	44
distractions	46
the blue rose	47
divine debris	49
a chardonnay life	50
shattered beauty	51
what you say yes to	52
create in the now	53
retreat	55
get out of the way	57
take your wetsuit off	59
release to each stroke	60
ancient yearning	62
what remains is love	63
show up for your life	64
bodypsalm for the earth	65
humus and humility	67
Celeste Snowber Profile	69
Dobee Snowber Profile	70

you are the earth

You know the story.
You have waited to come away for quite awhile.
It has carried you through all the details of your life
over and over again.
And you pack your bags, make all the travel
    arrangements and the hundreds of details to
    actually escape
    your home and work responsibilities.

You are a few days into your vacation
your holiday, which you thought would be a holy-day
turns out to be a rumble of your own soul.

You awake in the middle of the night to tsunami sirens.
You are robbed and mugged and your passport is gone.
You are still waiting for your baggage.
Waiting.

You are questioning.
But more importantly you awake
to an earthquake of your own spirit.
Everything that was secure before takes on a new lens.
You are ushered into seeing what matters and it is only this;

The sheer gift of life.

To breathe.
To smell.
To touch.
To hear.
To sense the waves of the sacred within you.
You are the earth
The earth is a body
And you are inextricably connected.

There is no rest as you thought for this vacation.
You are here to get the debris cleared
    the remnant of what does not matter.

This is what holidays are truly for.

To be with each moment
as a holy day.

wildness

You must not look to anyone to affirm your wildness
it is within you, given as your birthright.
It would be like the hibiscus or dandelion
asking if they were that flower.
You can never negate the flower you are.

Don' t look for the untame, the mysterious,
the unfathomable only on the outside.
The source is not at the volcano or waterfall.
The expression, yes,
the source is within you and hidden in all creation.
The volcano and waterfall choose to be their nature.
You must be yours.

Even as you write, the wind grasps your notebook
out of your hand and it flies onto the steps of the
lanai. Nothing is certain; outcomes or possibilities.
Staying true to your own nature is necessary.
The wind cannot deny its nature.
You have many natures within you.
And Mother Nature is always animating you
from the inside out.

plans

Plans are important.
You have one, in fact many. Small and large.
Plans for a grocery list, life list,
even plans of the heart.
Just know this: plans change
as destinations do.

You were planning to go to the store and
you arrived at the beach.
You plan to go to work and you
arrived home sick in bed.

The disturbance of your plans
is an ocean of new opportunity.
How else would the divine get your attention
but by changing your destination?

maps

Maps are necessary and precise.
You can Google map any location,
but you cannot Google map
the plan to your heart.
This journey you must traverse alone.
Even if you are in the company of many travellers
it is your unique path.
Only *you* can travel it.

Your path has its own textures, signposts,
curves and twists.
The signage may not be immediately apparent.
The signs are not always in colors you recognize.
You are looking for bold,
complementary colors: blue and orange.
The signs can be muted, in siennas and forest greens,
and change color with the lights.

Ripening the heart,
honing the intuition,
deep listening,
inward tenderness with fierce fire
are your tools for discerning the signs.

signs

The earth is always priming you
to notice light
within and without.
If you comprehend the external changes
noticing the outward weather
you will know the weather of your own journey.

Road signs are the same colors: yellow, red, green.
But the signs for your journey are:
magenta and plum.
aquamarine and cerulean.
burnt orange and crimson.

You are a child of many hues.

living exotically

There is a vast country waiting
within you to be discovered.
You don't even have to leave home
and there is a Fourth World country awaiting.
We speak of First and Third world and yet there is
still another world you have not visited.
Here no travel arrangements need to be made.

No airports, ferries or flight deals.
This is the supreme flight package;
flies directly to the delicious abyss *within* you
where true exoticism lies.
There are tastes, smells and sights
which are untold,
and only you can go on this trip.

There will be different species for each of you.
Be the explorer of your own inward travels.
Instead of just travelling to exotic places...

Live exotically.

the terrain of your own flesh

You love to buy a new holiday outfit; a dress, hat or
swim shorts as you embark
on going on your vacation.
Take a trip to the wonder of your own wild body.
Celebrate the curves and terrain of your own flesh.

Surprise yourself and get to know those parts of your
body you may want to cover up and give gratitude for

your skin sweating,
the release of tears,
deep belly laughs,
the sway of hips.

Your body is a flower
waiting to be opened and luxuriated in.
You take your precious body with you
wherever you go.
Your body is part of the earth and sea
already made up of 80% water.

Water is within you, without even leaving.
You *are* your body.

a tourist in your own life

You've had to compromise more than you
 understand.
Just to survive in this world has taken a toll.
You have been here for so long
you don't know what it feels like
to not come from a place of determination and
 action,
going from one task to another.
You have been the Queen Multitasker!

This is why you go on a holiday
and you are called to be a tourist in your own life.
To be a tourist in your life at home would be
to see from an observer's standpoint.
You would of course enjoy it more.

You'd be involved
but you wouldn't have to make it happen.
The day would unfold with a spice of grace.
Ease would be the main ingredient.

Do not turn your thoughts over and over again
place them in the hammock.
Let them swing from side to side
place them gently there
let ease be your companion.

a bagless life

Packing bags are what travellers do.
One would hope to carry only one
on the plane or on your back.
Lost baggage is always a risk
But the real reason to travel is to go away
so one can get rid of personal baggage.

On dating sites men often say in their profile,
"I have no baggage." First, that is incomprehensible
to really have no baggage.
Second, it's part of being human
that we all have some baggage.
The key to the baggage is whether
it is in the driver's seat.
Getting baggage out of the driver's seat
needs to be part of the flight plan.

One may not think there is baggage,
but all you have to do
is get irritated, triggered, jolted
and all the memories from the past swell up,
wash over you and there you are
sitting in the middle of your own mud.
I've done it many times myself,
and definitely have expertise in this area.

You know the scenario.
You came on vacation with your significant other, husband, wife, lover, friend, or family member and you are ready to leave him or her at the tourist booth and go off alone.
He or she is driving you nuts and you are in a funk.
Or it could even be yourself!
For the funk is within you,
and the other person just has the ability to excavate it. Really it is not even personal, but you think it is.

So this time, wherever you find yourself
take that baggage and just leave it.
Let the wind take the seeds within you, whatever it is, holding on, judgment, resentment, disappointment, injustice and let it clear out of you.

You will have room for more bags
and you will be both bagless and bag free.

raw joy

And then there is the tan.
You want one.
No doubt you need the vitamin D!
And your skin longs for radiance on its pores.

There is something else
that wants to be poured within you;
it is an inner radiance, streaming
from the inside out, dripping with a vitamin
that doesn't run out and combats stress
constantly.

RAW JOY is after you.
Within you. Over you. With you.
You've heard of raw food and its benefits.
Well this is the pure unadulterated freshness of joy.

This is different than happiness,
for happiness comes and go, as the sun does.
Rain always comes, just as you do
when joy rises within you.
But joy, is visceral and vibrates;
it is your inner tan.
You are tanned from the inside out.

Raw joy is with you whether you travel or not.
It is on the subway, in the car, in the kitchen,
bathroom, library, office, bedroom, or dentist chair.
Raw joy is a food group,
like chocolate and vegetables.

Pure sustenance.
Feed off it.
Grow it within you.
Nurture RJ.

But most of all
Live from *raw joy*.

where is she

So you might be wondering that I have said nothing
of the Divine Feminine; and this is from her.
Well, she comes in many forms,
and isn't relegated to a woman.
She is beyond wo/man, but has come
in the form of Pele, Mary, Black Madonna, and even
your neighborhood PTA woman, corporate gal
or absent minded, full-bodied professor.

She's all about embracing qualities that are
overlooked
as important:
unpredictability and fire.
water and ecstasy.
thunderous rolls and ocean spray.

She is tired of being relegated to back rooms
and so she appears in the night,
wakes you when you have let go
and wants to speak to you, tenderly,
with a flame that is inconsumable.

Listen to the sound of your skin
and the wine of your belly.
She wants to make you
ache with beauty once again.

The body sings

She wants the body to sing within you
so you re/member – re/body what
you knew deeply as a child:
the glorious grace
of dancing on the beach;
running in a pasture;
jumping into someone's arms;

being close to your feelings;
letting your emotions have their say
instead of pushing the delete button.

More than all this
is the sensate body
whatever shape, size,
limitation or asset you have:
the body sings.
the body cries and whispers
with a wash of wonder.

For too long you have been a tourist
in your own body,
sung another's song;
now is the time
to make home.

what about...

But you say what about...
my issue with body image, or this or
that, that or this.
There will always be a thousand obstacles.

Now is the time:
not after the diet
or after a resolution
or when the kids are gone
or when the divorce is done
or the marriage starts
or when you find someone
or the next job.

It only takes
small beginnings
the ingredients for small beauties.

Split an orange
and know the parts are as
beautiful as the whole.
The parts contain the whole
and the whole the parts.

one orange

One orange
has all the beauty,
all the juice and nourishment
of vitality waiting for you.

Who needs new couches, dresses,
cars or accessories if you cannot
luxuriate in the absolute
lusciousness of one orange?

And you are one wo/man,
one body soul heart mind
who has more miracles in
between your kidneys and fingers,
vagina and spleen,
eyes and ears
than any new home you could buy.

Come home
and come, come, come
in all the ways you can.

wired from the inside out

Connected.
The perpetual connection.
You want to flee
and at the same time you always want the option
to be able to connect in a moment.
Wired. Within and without.

Now is the time to be connected within and to
what is larger, the roaring, rolling, rumbling and
riotous divine feminine within.
Think of me as an infinite source of power,
your inner electricity
that never turns off, but turns you on.

Your cell phone may be out of range,
but the wired within is always in range,
and the beauty is, there are no roaming charges.
In fact, the wired within calls you to roam.
Roam into dreaming.
Follow your dreams.
Let them become uncovered
as you get rewired from the inside out.

I am enough
(or bodypsalm for superwo/man)

Enough is enough.
It is way too much doing, thinking, producing
and thinking about doing more
when it may be time to do less
be less and lessen; here is the lesson.
You have already produced more beauty,
generosity and work through one creative endeavor
or another for several lifetimes
not to mention children you have raised,
parents you have attended to,
gardens you have planted, literally and metaphorically;
and brought more people, projects and passions
to ripening than can be counted.
You are past counting
and now it is time to be countless
and perhaps be a countess.

Relax into a place of knowing
that you have already done enough
and now is the time to

S A V O R

Savor all the ways you have worked with your whole heart
and loved with your whole heart:
mothers, fathers, siblings, friends, children, lovers, spouses
and
even those who have left your life through natural or
unnatural causes.

Accept all your luxurious beauty of soulfulness that has
wrapped
around those you hold in your heart
and all the efforts you have made to follow meaning
in the world through work, words, worries and wantings.

Vibrate with all that is going through you;
the rise and fall of internal waves,
crashes of questions,
hormonal fluctuations in a sea of ripenings.

Own both your shortcomings and accomplishments
which means to name and rename what you truly
have done. Don't dismiss it in light of
living into the unknown.
Others own all your wonder. It is time for you to own it too.

Relinquish the need to be superwoman or superman.
Have a funeral for doing too much
and celebrate not doing in some way.
Enjoy being and know you are being formed into a wise one.

You are being called to drink from the cup of serene.
Each gesture is an act of love,
a counteraction to a world of overdoing,
an addiction to doing one more thing

when all along
the love in your eyes,
the way you behold who and what you love
is the fragrance of the One who gave
the beautiful scent of you.

inner mardi gras

There is an inner mardi gras within you.
You might have thought you had to travel
to New Orleans or the Caribbean
even though it is spectacularly wild,
colorful, sensuous, outrageous in every way;
but there is a music in your bones, so voluptuous
rhythmic that your whole body is one piece of jazz!

You can access it any time you want, even in times
of fasting from excess. This is an excess of soul
where spirit imbues you with beads of jubilation
and there is a necklace of unashamed festivity
guiding the inner recesses of your heart.

Call upon your mardi gras when needed.
If the flatlanders trouble you, know the
true wild/erness waits within,
always playing notes that are waiting to
be heard. This is a blues that never runs out.

hair or no hair – let it down

What is it about going on a vacation that you think
you must shave your legs, cut your hair, grow your
hair or get it right before you leave but
when you go to the cabin, you just let it go;
and who really cares?

It is time to let your hair go, be hairless,
hair free or at least free in the air.
You know that luxurious feeling when you really do
 "let your hair down"?
Well this really is a state of b e i n g;

a place where you descend into a deep relaxation,
rest, rest, rest; in the midst of dailiness.
I use to tell my three boys I would be a babe if I spent
as much time in the bathroom as they did on their hair.
They in turn told me, "Mom you need more product
in your hair."
Perhaps I did, to keep up with the times,
but I'm inviting you into living a more hair free life.

Try it; go outside with bad hair.
I'm doing it now.
No one seems to notice.
They still served my coffee
and I know I'm having a bad hair day,
so I can just live into it.
'Tis the season to take a vacation from hair.'

**live out loud from a deep
place of silence**

Always listen to your deep belly.
Here is where your voice resides.
Many will try to negate it in one way or
another, especially when it doesn't seem
rational, but there is another ration;
the ration of spirit,
where mystery and moss dwell
and the language of the impossible has reign.

There will be many times
where what you say
comes from a place from which you do not know;
yet you deeply know.
A familiar place of cellular knowledge.
Go there often.
Return as a place of home.
Resistance can become your friend
whether in the workplace or personal.
There is wisdom which does not make sense
but the earth knows intrinsically.
Your neck and heart will say yes
to an inner pulse.
Exercise it regularly.
Live out loud from a deep place of silence.

ripe tomato

You are a ripe, red, juicy tomato
waiting to be split open.
Honor the nature of the ripe tomato.
Notice the season you are in.
The one that is vine-ripened
is more delectable
than those that are forced to ripen.

Every passage you go through is
a part of your ripening;
the absolutely succulent growth
of growing in the fruit of a life.

A juicy existence is not neat,
cannot be confined,
splatters within the unexpected.
It has its own season,
both messy and magical.

Your juice is your life-force,
seeds of the tomato
spilling and splitting.
One only wants to drink its juices .
May you suck *ALL* the juice
out of life and celebrate raw beauty.

limits & liminality

Your limits
are the place of grace:
physical, spiritual, emotional,
mental or domestic.
You know how
to fix the leaky faucet, roof
or person in your life.

Knees are the weakest joints in the body.
All the more reason
to lie down and kayak.
There will always be parts of the journey
and parts of your body
which will prescribe a limit:
here is the place
to deeply embrace

and recognize the wisdom
in not having it perfectly together;
and actually allowing whatever is
to be the sacred space of acceptance
you are being invited
into; the place of in-between;
the liminality of creation
where dreams
are born and shed.

Here is the riparian zone
in between worlds.
The fertility of your own life
awaits. Trust,
nurture and celebrate
the incredible uniqueness
of limits
and liminality
awaiting.

fertility

Now is the time of the great fertility
and this is not about giving physical birth
but birth to the expanse of your own heart.
More than likely you are very good
at being responsible
or you wouldn't
be reading this book.

Fertility is the great response;
the luscious one of being alive
to whatever is growing within you
and having compassion to weeds,
worries, wanting's, whistling
waves and weather.

There was no way to prepare for
the mystery, magic and questioning
of your own life.
The result is internal weather.
The fruit:
fertility.

Do this: be kind and patient to all
which grows within you.

dreams and dreaming

Build a life that lets you dream
where waking and living are intertwined.
Ruminate on what is life-giving,
what haunts and propels you
into the knowing under the knowing.

Listen deeply to each image,
textures inside your dreams
both sleeping and awake.
Now is the time to dream more
honor and nurture them
as if they were babies
needing care and cuddles.

Your night dreams are a free meal.
50 visits to the therapist can be revealed in one dream.
Give them time, take them for supper,
a stroll, walk. Romance your dreams.

Here lies the secrets of your next steps
and the ushering in of your inner guides.
The creative soul requires dreams
as you need dark chocolate;
and your bodyspirit aches
to be dreamed and dream.

dark chocolate

What you long for is often good for you
but you only accept its longing when some
statistic verifies what you knew all along.
Dark chocolate is an example.

You might have always loved it;
the rich brown color and taste dissolving
in your mouth; your taste buds going
into a full explosion of YES!

Now it is acknowledged: it has health benefits,
antioxidants; antidote to depression.
Here is the lesson:
listen with your taste buds. Let them guide you
into a knowing. Your body will tell you what
you need. Ripe with wisdom,
tongue knowing,
let your palate find your way
to the next meal of your heart.

tears

Tears are food too;
a power drink with a pinch of salt
straight from your innermost being
to the flesh on your face

tears are your liquid jewels.
To have your joy, you
must have your sorrow,
the invitation in the
practice of release;

and here is your new lease
stemming from an eternal
hot spring within.

You know how you love
hot springs; the healing
quality of minerals on your body.
Your tears are
your warm springs
for your capacity
to live deeply.

These too are prayers.

living into the not yet

Ponder why
you are so attracted
to unopened tulips:
luscious red, yellow and orange
petals proclaiming attention
standing on the verge
of an opening
encased; as if pearls
had a life inside.

Notice interior time;
the shy one within you
calling, searching you out
in the whispers beneath
bringing you back
to a patience of
living into the not yet.

rehearkening

Hearken back to what you
knew in the beginning
when you were prompted
by the still small voice;
the rush of wind in your chest
prodding you back to another way;
the way of the mystic and fool;
the one who plays in the dark
and dances in the light
seeing the unseeing
of the bulb in the soil.

You know the other place
where you are enlivened
and all things are new.

Remember.
Rebody
the simplicity of the deep.
Wait for the elegant lines
drawing into you.
Rehearken, rehear, reheart.

a riot of color

You know what you know.
What is it that you don't know?
The place of unforeseen
isn't this why you love improvisation.

In life it is different.
You still want to have some security;
the familiarity of what is known.

It is the unfamiliar which is exotic.
You don't have to travel
to a tropical climate.

The unknown is a bed of petals
anticipating your arrival,
softening into a different destination.
You have departed from the known
and you are on the runway of new starts.
Here are no forgotten wings
only material to glide.

This is the province of trust:
simply,
quietly,
a riot of color.

in-between of travelling

You live in the place
where you are home
and not at home in this world
and not of this world.
This is the state of being human
for we come from somewhere.
We live in the where
and we don't know
where we are going.

We are in the state of travelling
the province of traversing,
whether you step on a plane
or go on a trip,
our lives are a continual trip
from one point to another
and this is not pointless,

for it is the place of in-between
where ripeness lies.
The heart lies open to be discovered,
over and over again,
peeled back as the fresh apple.

You are being called to be peeled back.
Be under the skin and let the skin off.

Honor the spaces in your life
where you are caught in between;

between health and unhealthy,
singleness and coupledom,
employment and unemployment,
peace and hesitation.

All is the journey
and this *is* what we were made for.
We are constantly wanting to arrive,
yet arrival happened as soon as
you departed from your mother's womb;
and you have also been departing
since you arrived.

Travel tip:
luxuriate in the trip of your own
exquisite life
as only you know.

distractions

Notice your distractions.
They are the hints of what
your heart yearns for
and calls you back to.

The distraction is the attraction
where magic plays out;
an unraveling
of what could delight you in the belly
under the skin, on the tip of your lips.

Remember your most magical times in your life.
They could never have been planned
so here in this moment
STOP
and notice what halts you to attention.

It may be the falling leaf
but it could also be who gives you life
and who drains you;
or another path searching you out.
Instead of thinking that its you who is finding,
know the distractions will find you
and here you will be found.

the blue rose

What has been said to be impossible
is the entry to only what is possible
paradox at the door.

You don't see roses that are blue
but that is what you are:
a blue rose.
Everyone said it could not be done
but you knew better.
Remember the time
that is nestled within your heart
where a small infinity was birthed,
spilled over and created the uniqueness
of what you truly hold dear.

*You know what I am talking about
and yes, it is different for each of you.*

So gather your impossibilities
as burnt orange leaves on the ground;
scoop them up and release
them in the bowl for birthing.

These are the days to turn
over the soil and see

obstacles as compost
for growing what is unimaginable...
a blue rose

divine debris

You are in love with debris
colored beach glass
hues of greens and lavender
admist the whites and browns
random art at the shore.

Scattered leaves bled
with hints of orange and red
chestnuts shining on the ground
winter and fall coming together
as lovers, spread on the earth.

Seasons intermingle
a time warp
pine cones and driftwood
branches and lilacs
all returning to the soil
your heart; the land.

Each turning over its fertility
to bring a fresh beginning
divine debris
ingredients for what is to come.

a chardonnay life

You know the feeling.
By the time you embark
on your holiday time
you are utterly exhausted,
depleted and deleted;
and you are too tired to proceed.
What you yearn for
is a vacation from the holiday
and a holiday from the vacation.

Vacating your own life;
vacating to your real life;
what is real in the first place?

Remember the first sip of chardonnay
on a summer's evening?
Fruit, ripened, sweet, lingering,
a shallot of grape,
this is the taste of your inner sweetness.
Return to your chardonnay life
and celebrate your inner grape
waiting to be ripened by
your deep attention.

shattered beauty

The wine glass breaks
shatters all over the wood floor
hundreds of pieces vacate
what once could contain your merlot.

Nothing is left to hold you
or wine for that matter
but you are the wine of your life
robust red rolling in the hills
of your own voluptuousness.

You pick up the pieces
what was broken
remnants what held promise
sweep into memory.

Begin again to crush the grapes
of desire and know shattering
is the birth of a nascent chance
to once again see clearly
the life that yearns to live.

what you say yes to

You will be asked over and over again
"Do you know how to say no?"
as if you have not learned this lesson
over and over again; after all, how do you
think you got through careers, children,
relationships, strangers...you have learned
to say no, but the real question is...

"What do you say yes to?" And I am not talking
about all the responsibilities that are on your
shoulders in one form or another.
If you are reading this book you are already more than
responsible, which is different than responsive.

N o t i c e:
what you say yes to and
how you can say yes *MORE* to
what gives you life, animates you, feeds you,
nourishes your soul, body, mind, senses, and feet.

So instead of thinking about what we say no to,
be invited to respond to what calls forth to say YES
and this is the place for you to dwell;
so take yourself on a retreat!

create in the now

Living boldly cannot be contained
presence asks to be listened to
drawn, danced, desired
in the cracks of life
if one waits to create ~
time will be finite.

Seize the moment
for each second calls forth new colors
textures and poems, songs and stories
to break forth from the splits
in our busy schedules
of comings and goings, pick ups and drop offs,
emails and calls & important agendas.

Create in the now
in small beauties
where ten minutes can transform a day
a turn of the heart towards art
is all it takes to see
again for the first time
and hear symphonies in birdsong
movements in waterfall.

The pulsing body within you
asks for new hues in your life

break open the oranges and purples
celebrate green and yellows
let scars be imprints of soul
interruptions be compositions of wonder.

Create in the cracks
and here lies words and worlds
the autobiography of clouds
formations of spirit
split into
one more possibility.

retreat

What is it in that word that you
do not get; it is a treat for you!
Designed for you to treat yourself
and be able to be the wild tourist
in your own life.
The duties of the
world can eat up your wildness.
Instead of living in your own wilderness,
your life begins to feel domesticated
from every perspective.

Wildness is:
seeing, hearing,
touching, listening
as if for the first time.
Primavera.
First sight.
Where you look at a worn piece of sea glass,
and see the horizon, and light
shimmering on water it's enough.
The smallest things can give you pleasure.
The retreat
is waiting within you
but sometimes you must
leave, catapult yourself
away from the everyday of your own life.

One does not need to go far.

Treats abound.
It is the apple pie of your life
waiting for *YOU*.

get out of the way

The best thing you can do for yourself
is to get out of the way.
You actually have become so competent
even though you might argue to the contrary
that you are easily deceived to think
that *you* have to get yourself out of every predicament,
solve every problem,
troubleshoot and manage
more issues, details, friends, family or
personal deliberations than is possible.
So just remember:
>   you can't do it all.
>   you can't even do what you want
>   and what you want is revealed
>   by letting life happen.

No need
to keep pushing the river;
let the river push you
and pull you into its flow.

Get out of the way
and see
the delicious wonder of the earth;
and the spirit and the feminine holding you,
dancing with you

on this journey.

Release to becoming less
so you can become more;
and you know in your cells
what it means to be carried.

take your wetsuit off

Take your wetsuit off
and experience
the glorious sensuality of being alive
in your senses, water soaked.
This is the gift
from the Creator.
The earth is the essence of creation,
has the scent of the divine
on its skin
awaiting to be on your skin.

Why swim a warm lake in a wet suit?
The exhilaration of water
cannot enter your pores.
The masks, personas, or being guarded
prevent the miraculous to enter
your moist being.

Naked to the world,
naked to your breath,
naked to god in you
and you in god and the
elements that wait
to pulsate inside your skin.

release to each stroke

Release to each stroke
as a practice for life
let liquid suspend you
float into time.

Be renewed
in the water of existence
where floating is a spiritual practice
and the rhythm of swimming
is the way of daily baptism
where concerns lie in the past.

Plunge your limbs into the present
speed or slowness does not matter
in the great pool
you are buoyed by lightness
muscles and joints work effortlessly.

Here is the metaphor
for traversing your path
simplicity of backstroke
the sky is your focus
repetition is a hymn.

Swim to a gliding life
splash into mystery
body stretching
to the next moment.

ancient yearning

You are the language of stars
torsos spinning in light
primal songs
reside in your flesh.

Commune with the infinite
underbelly of the heart
let what you long for
come to the surface.

Trees and tears are prayers
creation resides within
ancient beginnings
yearning for home.

what remains is love

Your heart gets left at the airport
you drop off your son, lover, daughter,
mother, friend, spouse
they leave for the land they must live in
and you are a thousand miles away.

Gone are the days we all dwell in the same place
beloved ones are flung like constellations
of suns and moons thrown apart
skies and bonds of unbroken singing.

Arrivals and departures
two choices at terminals
but beloved ones are always
arriving and departing in the space
inside the body's love
reaching far beyond any destination
of a world round trip.

You carry within
those you nurture and are nurtured by
in the suitcase of your soul
waiting for the next time
to enter the portal of homecoming.

What remains is love.

show up for your life

Release into the life
that wants to be lived in you.

Not the one you planned
but the one least expected
yet matches the call of your longing.

Let gentle whispers
and bold beginnings
of unmeasured time
rip through your veins
announcing unfettered joy.

Sparkle with purpose
of your own interior design.

Show up for your own life
waiting beneath the skin of you.

bodypsalm for the earth

The earth is shaking within its core
and our cores in turn are shaken
now is the season to wake up
from the inside out
proclaim the interconnection
to all living beings -
neighbours near and far
sun, stars, sea, plants and plankton
and most of all
the fertile earth
which both gives and takes away.

May we return to humility
where humus, humans and humour are born
and taste the mystery and beauty
beneath our feet and bellies.

May our limbs stretch to the sky
our soles/souls kiss the ground
and may hope soak
our minds and bodies
through changes of weather
both of the heart and land.

May we bear grace in our bones
and be rebodied to the truth -

our flesh is the earth
and the earth is our flesh.

May compassion arise from our well
as we return to the fire of love
which has the capacity
to hold more than we know.

humus and humility

Underneath the fault lines
here lies the journey
required for the wild tourist
there are no trains, planes, cycles
or fast tracks for arrival.

Last night before sleeping
on the 2nd to last day of the year
I asked to be guided
to listen to what else
asked to be voiced
in this book living within me.

Tossing into unrest
I jolted from slumber
body shaking
into my first earthquake
4.9 on the scale.

What instrument of measurement
reveals the earthquake of spirit?

Humus and humility are partners
we are the wild earth
the wild earth is in us.

Celeste Snowber
Dance & Performance Artist, Writer, Educator,

Celeste Snowber, Ph.D. is a dancer, writer, poet and educator, who is an Associate Professor in the Faculty of Education at Simon Fraser University, Greater Vancouver, BC Canada. Her essays and poetry have been published extensively in various journals and chapters in books and she is author of *Embodied Prayer* and co-author of *Landscapes in Aesthetic Education*. Her deep love of place has informed both her performative and poetic work and she continues to create and perform site-specific dance and poetry in connection to the natural world. She has performed a full-length show including dance, humor and voice entitled, *"Women giving birth to a red pepper,"* which explores sexuality and mid-life. Celeste has three amazing adult sons and lives in New Westminster, B.C. with her husband. Her website can be found at www.celestesnowber.com and blog at www.bodypsalms.com.

Dobee Snowber
Artist

Dobee Snowber is a working Artist, (printmaking, painting and mixed media), making time between time and whenever possible, to create. She has lived in the San Francisco Bay area for 17 years. Prior to that time she lived in Santa fe and before that various and sundry places east of the Rockies. Dobee holds a BA in Intellectual History/Feminist Studies from Kirkland College and a BFA in Printmaking and Painting from the Maine College of Art in Portland, Maine. She has shown extensively in various venues including galleries, museums, group collaborations and solo exhibits. She currently shows @ Mary Praytor Gallery in Greenville, SC. Dobee, her partner Clare, and their 2 children, Jesse and Michael, reside in Berkeley. More of her work can be found at dobeesnowber.squarespace.com.

Dobee and Celeste are currently collaborating on a book of Celeste's bodypsalms and Dobee's images.